The Great Flood of Dusty Plains

Written by Mary-Anne Creasy

Illustrated by Stephen Axelsen

Flying Start
to Literacy®

T0363477

Contents

Chapter 1:
Ready Ron

In the little town of Dusty Plains, it had not rained for years and years. But Ron, the town's safety officer, was ready. Ron was always ready.

He was ready for every possible disaster –
bushfires, cyclones, earthquakes . . .
and floods, if it ever rained. He was ready
with his boat so he could help people.

"It's not going to rain, Ron," said his
neighbour Molly. "You should put that
boat away."

But Ron just shook his head.
"You never know, you just never know."

That very day, on the radio, there was an urgent message. A huge storm was coming. It was going to rain. It was going to rain for a week.

"We have to get ready for a flood," said Ron.

"It won't rain," said the mayor to Ron. "Don't worry."

"They've been saying for years that it will rain," said the police chief, "and it never does!"

"There won't be a flood," said Molly, "because it's not going to rain."

But Ron got the boat ready anyway.

"You never know, you just never know," he said.

Ron went to the town hall. He collected the town's most important things and put them in his boat.

First, he put in the photograph of the King with all the townspeople.

Next, he put in the town's prize-winning pumpkin.

Then he put in the dinosaur bone that the mayor's grandfather had discovered.

The last things to go in Ron's boat were food, water and a first-aid kit.

"If the town hall floods, all the important things will be saved," he said.

Chapter 2:
Rain, rain, rain!

Then something happened. A drop of rain plipped onto the dusty ground. Then came another drop.

"Rain!" said Ron.
"Rain!" said the police chief.
"Rain!" said the mayor.

The rain fell faster and faster. Everyone
rushed home, out of the rain.

Ron put his biggest umbrella over the boat.
He was ready. He sat on his veranda and
watched the rain.

It rained all that day and all the next day. It rained all week. The water in the river rose higher and higher.

Then it happened – the water in the river flowed over the banks. Muddy water flowed into the town. The flood had come.

Finally, the rain stopped. Ron got into his
boat and rowed through the streets, looking
for people who needed help.

Chapter 3:
Ron to the rescue

Ron rowed past the mayor's house.

"Help, Ron, help!"

Ron looked up. There was the mayor, sitting on the roof of her house.

"Can I get in your boat, Ron?" asked the mayor.

"I'll have to make space for you," said Ron.
He looked at all the town's most important
things. He picked up the photograph of the
King with the townspeople and threw it
into the water.

Splash!

The mayor climbed down from the roof
and into the boat.

Ron and the mayor rowed through more streets. They rowed past the police chief's house. He had climbed up a tree.

"Help, Ron, please help me!" he said. "Please, let me in your boat."

Ron looked at all the town's most important things.

"I'll have to throw out two things to fit you in," he said.

Ron picked up the town's prize-winning pumpkin and the dinosaur bone and tossed them into the water.

Splash! Splash!

Ron, the mayor and the police chief watched them float away. The police chief then climbed down from the tree and into the boat.

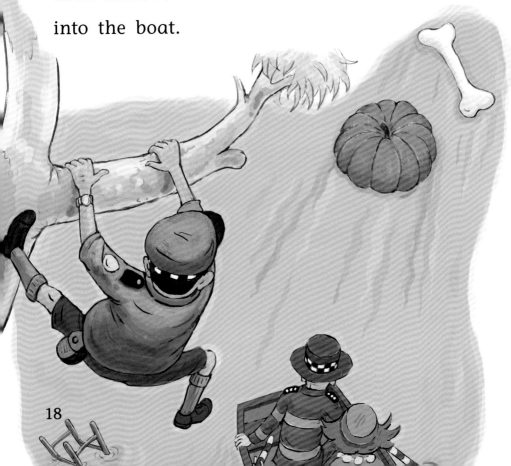

18

"What about Molly?" said the police chief.

"Molly! We've got to get Molly!" said Ron.

Ron rowed as fast as he could to Molly's house.

Chapter 4
Where's Molly?

When they reached Molly's house, they all called out, "Molly, Molly, we've come to save you."

But there was no answer. The door of Molly's house was open and the floodwaters were inside.

"Oh, no!" said Ron. "Where is she?"

Just then, they heard a shout. They turned
and there was Molly. She was paddling a
boat. She paddled towards them.

As Molly got closer, Ron saw that her boat was packed full . . .

There was the photograph of the King, the town's prize-winning pumpkin and the dinosaur bone!

"I thought these things were important,"
said Molly, "so I saved them."

"But where did you get the boat?"
asked Ron.

"Oh, I've had this for ages," said Molly.
"Because you never know, Ron, you just
never know. It's good to be ready!"

A note from the author

This story is based on what happened in south-east Queensland after a long drought in 2004–10. No rain had fallen in this area for a very long time and many dams had dried up.

Then, suddenly, it began to rain, and it rained heavily. Many towns flooded. The people in these towns were not prepared and the floods caused lots of damage.

In my story, the townspeople of Dusty Plains laughed at Ron because he was preparing for a flood, which they thought would never happen. But being prepared for any emergency is actually a smart thing to do, because you just never know!